THE GOLDEN BOOK
HAVANA

Text by Renato Recio, Eduardo Jiménez *and* Milena Recio

BONECHI
EDITORIAL
José Martí

© Copyright by CASA EDITRICE BONECHI
Via Cairoli 18b - 50131 Florencia, Italia
Tel. 055/576841 - Fax 055/5000766
E-mail: bonechi@bonechi.it - Internet: www.bonechi.it
ISBN 88-476-0149-5

© EDITORIAL JOSÉ MARTÍ
Publicaciones en Lenguas Extranjeras
Apartado Postal 4208
La Habana 10400, Cuba
Tel. (537)333541 / 329838 - Fax (537)333441 / 338187
E-mail: cclfilh@artsoft.cult.cu
ISBN 959-09-0154-9

Project: CASA EDITRICE BONECHI
Editorial Director: Monica Bonechi
Graphic Design: Serena de Leonardis
Picture Research: Serena de Leonardis
Editing: Magaly Silva *and* Giovannella Masini
Video Page Making: Fiorella Cipolletta
Cover: Laura Settesoldi
Texts: Renato Recio, Eduardo Jiménez *and* Milena Recio
Translation: Richard Dunbar

The photographs contained in this volume, taken by
Marco Bonechi *and* Paolo Giambone
are property of the Casa Bonechi Editrice Archives.

Printed in Italy by
CENTRO STAMPA EDITORIALE BONECHI

Introduction

Contrary to what some might think, Cuba has been a land of many discoveries over the centuries. In fact, before Christopher Columbus reached its shores on October 28, 1492, the island had already been visited by "foreigners": natives most probably coming from the Caribbean mainland, who, in the course of their explorations, had often sailed towards this new land seeking fair shores on which to settle. It is possible to imagine that these "indios"—as Columbus called them in the belief he had reached India—lived peacefully, surrounded by a nature that provided all their needs for a sustainable life. The European discovery of the New World, dividing the earth into hemispheres, ended the peaceful existence of the original inhabitants, marking the start of five centuries of history that up until present times has also been, in different ways and in different moments, a history of encounters with Cuba.

It was especially Cuba's status as an island and its privileged location in the Caribbean Sea that made the land attractive. The warm temperatures and tropical rains have shaped a landscape that is remarkable for its variety and uniqueness. This virgin and fertile nature seduced not only Columbus, who stated, "This is the most beautiful land that human eyes have ever seen." German naturalist and geographer Alexander von Humboldt (1769-1859), who was considered the second discoverer of Cuba, provided the first scientific description of its fascinating mountains, endless beaches and the variety of its flora and fauna. Linked to the island's nature, which had so impressed Columbus and Humboldt, was another discovery that would prove to be even more important.

Between 1920 and 1950, ethnologist and author Don Fernando Ortiz made an in-depth examination of the most intimate secrets of that impalpable and complex atmosphere that had developed over the centuries, which came to be known as cubanía. The scientist, born in his beloved Havana, the Cuban capital, thus earned for himself the title of the third discoverer of the island.

If Columbus had revealed to the world the existence of Cuba, and Humboldt had described the land, Ortiz was able to sketch its profile, defining the Cubans as the most generous fruit of this land, and their boasting of it as their greatest quality. Through a complex process, which Ortiz called "transculturation," the inhabitants of Cuba evolved in a world apart and sprung from diverse ethnic roots, with the white Spaniards and other Europeans who emigrated to

The Malecón, Havana's popular seafront avenue.

Cuba mixing with the black Africans, brought to the island as slaves starting in 1526.

The mulatto, which refers not only to the color of skin, expresses one of the most important symbols of Cubanía, a fusion of diverse cultures that has created its own identity. Under the Cuban sun, which beat down with equal intensity on the Spanish merchant, the Creole proprietor and the African slave, the diverse religious beliefs, customs and many psycho-social differences of all the inhabitants melted together in a particular syncretism, even despite the barriers erected by the white dominion and Catholicism.

Other nationalities, though not predominating in Cuba, have by their mere presence contributed their own characteristics and participated in the creation of this fusion that makes up the Cuban identity. Among them have been the Chinese, brought to the island and subjected to slavery, the French and Haitians, who came when they fled the bloody Haitian Revolt of 1791 and promoted, among other things, the cultivation of coffee in the east of the country, and the North Americans, present in the country since the 18th century. There has even been an Arab contribution, which had exerted influence on the Spanish culture over the centuries.

Cuba has always had an ambiguous relationship with the seas that surround it. From them came the conquerors, pirates and corsairs, the cyclones and hurricanes, and the slaves; they also brought scientific discoveries and such technologies as the printing press, the steam engine and the railroad. Because of the constant action of the waves, vast sandy white beaches developed, gently sloping into the clear waters of the bays that abound on the island's long coastline.

From across the sea also arrived, at the end of the 19th century, the United States navy, with the mission of intervening in the Spanish-Cuban conflict, but in reality interfering with the real independence of Cuba. And disembarking on the south coast in 1956 were the 82 young Cubans led by Fidel Castro, who once again took up the struggle for the sovereignty of their country, a half republic since 1902 and governed by the interests of the United States of America. Surround entirely by water, buffeted on all sides by winds, the object of countless foreign passions, oppressions, conceits and plots, the island and its inhabitants finally became their own masters with the historic event that radically revolution-

ized the political, social and cultural life of Cuba. The 1959 triumph granted the people a heretofore unknown dignity, which itself generated new energies and other unknown quantities contributing to the Cuban personality and identity.

The city of Havana, whose history since its beginnings has gone hand in hand with the history of Cuba, still continues to be one of the places that best exemplifies the memories of the past and the excitement of modern times, Cuban style.

Among the elegant buildings from past centuries, saved thanks to a keen interest for the preservation of their heritage, and old American cars, whose impressive numbers testify to their unusual mechanical longevity, the Habaneros, like most Cubans, demonstrate what they have lived through and what they have adapted to: that which they themselves call the "culture of resistance."

Living in a paradoxical dialectic of survival and development, of immobility and international leadership, the Cubans have developed into one of the most interesting peoples in the world, especially if one considers that the country is neither particularly large nor populous.

But the mystery of Cubanía reveals itself with difficulty. The question, "What is a Cuban like?" can be answered in a thousand different ways, many of them contradictory. Lively and extroverted, profound and tenacious, able to joke even in the most difficult situations and ready for sacrifice and extreme abnegation. While not neglecting their prevalently sensual side, they are romantics and pragmatics, patriots and cosmopolitan, austere and spendthrift ...

As soon as we meet a Cuban, many adjectives come to mind in describing him. However, there are still no precise words for a people who, despite their short time as a nation, have been at the forefront of so much history, have faced such powerful enemies and have dreamed in such an enormously impassioned way.

Modern Havana, seen from the sea.

The Cathedral, one of the symbols of Havana.

OLD HAVANA

Near the spot once known as Puerto de Carenas, a group of men, following the currents of the Gulf of Mexico, decided to found the fifth settlement on the island of Cuba on the basis of the colonization plan drawn up by the conquistador Diego Velázquez. It was the third attempt of these men, led by Pánfilo de Narváez, to find a suitable place for the settlement. They first looked near the mouth of a river on the south coast. Then they moved towards the north coast, near the mouth of a river today called the Almendares. They then went to a hospitable bay, well protected by the fury of the ocean, which would become the point of convergence for all the ships that traveled between Spain and her American colonies. The village built on the bay became with time a populated city, rich in history and culture.

The original area of present day Havana, known as Old Havana, and in particular its famed historic center, declared a Heritage Site for Humanity by UNESCO in 1982, is made up of numerous buildings, plazas,

churches, parks and streets. This old city center recounts the story of a culture that was formed by a unique mix of Spanish, African and American (in the true sense of the word), and its special charm makes it the most popular spot for the hundreds of thousands of tourists who visit the Cuban capital every year.

The buildings along the narrow but well laid-out streets, though not reaching the architectural levels of those built in Europe between the 15th and 19th centuries, create a unique grace that represents, as described by one of the main scholars of Cuban architecture, the most accomplished and personal exemplification of colonial architecture. The functional architectural design of these buildings provides remarkable testimony to the country's society, life and customs, and demonstrate the variety of materials that the island's inhabitants have produced from their land and their industry over the ages.

This architecture helps to create the special atmosphere that one breathes in throughout much of the

historic center, which covers some 150 hectares. In the 1950s, the construction of the bay tunnel, which led to the development of the city around Old Havana, increased the land value in this area to such a degree that the people who most ardently promoted the preservation of the country's cultural heritage came under serious threat. The fear turned into reality when plans were announced for the construction of a heliport on the grounds of the oldest university in Cuba.

With the Cuban Revolution of 1959, this trend, which would have virtually destroyed Old Havana, was fortunately halted, and the buildings in this section of the city were converted for governmental and commercial use.

Today, taking advantage of the swift growth in tourism, new ideas are being studied for the financing of the costly works of restoration and preservation of the historic center: government funds have been earmarked to carry out these works, and the Oficina del Historiador de La Habana (The Havana National Historical Society) has been instituted for the collection and disbursement of the funds.

La Plaza de Armas

Although the five original plazas created at the dawn of the urbanization of Havana are still preserved, the Plaza de Armas continues to provide natural access to the historic center. At the beginning of the 16th century, the Plaza and the surrounding area made up the first nucleus of San Cristóbal de La Habana, the point where the wide bay of Havana and the natural canal that connects it with the open sea meet and where the first colonizers settled. The Plaza de Armas is therefore the oldest of Havana's squares, and it was the center of the lives of the founders of the early village. At the far eastern side of the square is El Templete (the Temple), a small Neo-Classical building erected in 1828 to mark the spot where in 1519 the first mass was held and where the first *Cabildo* (government) operated, in the shade of the giant *ceiba* tree.

In the middle of Plaza de Armas, the statue of Carlos Manuel de Céspedes, called the "Father of the Nation" for being the courageous initiator of the armed fight for national independence.

Used book vendors are an integral part of Plaza de Armas.

El Templete stands out among the colonial buildings that surround Plaza de Armas, constructed to perpetuate the memory of the first mass and the first Cabildo in the city.
In the photo, the building during restoration.

Important buildings dating from the colonial era around Plaza de Armas. Among them is the Palacio del Segundo Cabo. In front of its large and shaded archways can be found stands of used book vendors and artisans.

From Plaza de Armas, looking north, stands the Palacio del Segundo Cabo, built in 1772 as the Real Casa de Correos (Royal Post Office).

The small courtyard of the Palacio del Segundo Cabo features lowered arches supported by columns and pedestals, constituting a Classical stylistic composition of Adalusian inspiration.

Inside of the elegant Neo-Classical memorial are still the frescoes by the French painter Jean-Baptiste Vermay, who reproduced the inauguration of the Templete and the first mass. The Habaneros have always ensured that next to the Templete a ceiba has grown, and every year on the day commemorating the founding of the city they circle the tree in silence three times so that three wishes they make to Saint Christopher, protector of Havana, come true.

The Plaza de Armas was originally named Plaza de la Iglesia (Plaza of the Church), since it was the custom during the times of Spanish colonization to place the parish church in the area where the main citizens of the new village lived. In that period, however, the dwellings, like the church, were humble *bohíos*, rustic buildings like those of the natives. The site began to lose its original name when the *Castillo de la Real Fureza* (Castle of the Royal Army) was built, another of the main elements still visible along the square. The garrison stationed in the castle often used the adjoining square to carry out their drills and maneuvers, so that around 1580 the people began calling the square Plaza de Armas.

Much time passed before the original plaza took on its final appearance, and it was only in the last third of the 18th century, after Havana was taken over by the English and the city and the island were affected by new economic impulses that changed the policies of the royal administration, that the site was adorned with fountains, trees and decorations. This was also the period in which the surrounding streets were graced with monumental buildings symbolizing Spanish colonial prowess: the Palacio de los Capitanes Generales (Palace of General Captains, or the Palace of Government) and the Palacio del Segundo Cabo (Palace of the Second Chief or the General Vice-Captain), both today perfectly preserved. From this period, the chroniclers and travelers began to leave frequent testimony of the importance of Plaza de Armas during the colonial era.

The entrance to the main stairway, located at the rear of the courtyard of the Palacio del Segundo Cabo, was designed to produce a strong sense of depth.

The mixed-line arch of the entry to the main stairway of the Palacio del Segundo Cabo.

Partial view of the facade of the Palacio de los Capitanes Generales. The palace was begun in 1796 and completed in 1834. Note the roof terrace with iron railings interrupted by crenellations.

Elegant carriages continually circled the plaza, carrying the aristocratic women of Havana, while the men strolled in the park or sat on benches, awaiting a discreet glance or a prudent greeting from a woman on the verge of falling in love. This era provided the prints that served as models for the restoration of the plaza in 1935, bringing it back to its appearance of 1841.

Whoever strolls in Plaza de Armas today sees not only the faithful reproduction of its original layout and of the buildings that remain around its edges. They can also enjoy the musical bands that perform concerts in the same spot that military marches once took place. In the surrounding area it is still possible to see an occasional horse carriage pass by, driven by a liveried coachman, while lovely women walk through the park in 19th century dress.

Palacio del Segundo Cabo

The Palacio del Segundo Cabo, as it has come to us from the 19th century, was built starting in 1772 in a measured Baroque style, a manifest prelude to the Neo-Classical. Located in the northern section of the plaza, near the Castillo de la Real Fuerza, the Palacio was originally the Real Casa de Correos (Royal Post Office). Subsequently, it was the seat of the Real Intendencia de Hacienda, until the colonial era ended and it became the residence of the Segundo Cabo in 1854. Now the building houses the Cuban Book Institute and every day, at the opening of its majestic door, decorated by huge and elegant pilasters, one can catch a glimpse of its square arcaded patio whose columns and pedestals reveal its Andalusian origins.

Palacio de los Capitanes Generales
(Municipal Museum)

The Palacio de los Capitanes Generales was several years after the Palacio del Segundo Cabo, using the same local limestone that was used for the former in order to maintain stylistic harmony. The Casa de Gobierno (Government Palace), which also reflects a sort of Classical Baroque in its facade and in much of its interior, occupies all of the western side of the Plaza de Armas and is today the home of the Municipal Museum and of the Oficina del Historiador de La Habana (Havana National Historical Society).
The Municipal Museum contains an extremely rich account of Cuban history in the splendid setting of the antique palace of the Spanish governors, who from the balcony watched the nighttime military parades that took place in the plaza, which reached its splendor with the construction of these two buildings.

The statue of Christopher Columbus, by Italian sculptor J. Cucchiari, was placed in the beautiful courtyard of the Palacio de los Capitanes Generales in 1862.

Baroque style arcades look out onto the central courtyard of the Palacio de los Capitanes Generales.

Dominated by sets of medallóns (Isabellean furniture with wicker added to suit the Cuban climate), this 19th-century style room of the Municipal Museum recreates the lifestyle of the Creole aristocracy.

Known as the Music Salon, this was the ante-chamber of the main hall of the Palacio de los Capitanes Generales. Visitors can admire the emblem of the monarchy (foreground) and of the city. On the central table are two 18th-century Meissen porcelain vases.

The Green Room was originally the ante-chamber of the public office of the Capitanes Generales. The furnishings and rug are original.

The Main Hall. The original 19th-century Venetian mirrors witnessed, among many important events, the end of Spanish dominion in 1899 and the entry into power of the president of the Republic in 1902.

Guéridon Table from the 19th century. The images are of Napoleon and his generals. The table was in the Kuquine property of the dictator Fulgencio Batista, from where it was brought to the Municipal Museum.

Throne Hall of the Palacio de los Capitanes Generales. The hall was built for the Spanish royalty out of respect and subordination, although no royalty ever came to Cuba. Small receptions were given by the General Captain in this hall.

Wicker furniture in the Municipal Museum reached Cuba at the end of the 19th century, and Art Nouveau at the beginning of the 20th century.

This salon is known as the Coffee Room, a beverage that became over time a fixture in the life of Cuban families. The display case to the right holds a collection of valuable fans produced with precious materials such as coral, mother of pearl, ivory, amethyst and emeralds.

The bath of the Palacio de los Capitanes Generales, containing two original large marble bathtubs. The screens are also of great value.

The first Flag Hall of the Municipal Museum, containing the three most important flags in the history of Cuba and flags of the nations that supported the island in its fight for independence. The Hall also holds the uniform of Máximo Gómez and one of the machetes used in battle by Antonio Maceo, two key figures in Cuban history.

One of the many treasures housed in the Municipal Museum: the flag raised by Carlos Manuel de Céspedes at Demajague to mark the beginning of the Ten Year War in 1868.

The second Flag Hall of the Municipal Museum. On the right are the combat flags carried by the Mambí army; on the left are the flags of the patriot associations that supported the struggle from abroad. In the display cases are objects that testify to the most important events of the War of Independence.

In the rear of the second Flag Hall, The Death of Maceo, an oil painting by Armando Menocal.

Oil portraits of the patriots of the War of Independence in the Municipal Museum. This collection by Federico Martínez contains 110 paintings from the beginning of the 20th century.

The brick pavement of the Plaza de la Cathedral hosts the stands of artisans selling their crafts.

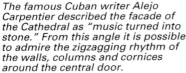

This side view of the great Havana church does not make its suggestive Baroque facade any less majestic.

The famous Cuban writer Alejo Carpentier described the facade of the Cathedral as "music turned into stone." From this angle it is possible to admire the zigzagging rhythm of the walls, columns and cornices around the central door.

The Cathedral and Plaza

For a very long period, the development of colonial architecture in Cuba and Havana depended substantially on the kind of economy that Spain established on the island when it was realized that no gold or gems would be found there.

For much of the period, the economic life of Cuba was marked by self-sufficiency, with the exception of Havana, whose main source of wealth depended on the great traffic of ships, forming large fleets that linked the New World with the main Spanish ports. This role of the capital, and the fact that is was constantly under the threat of pirates and corsairs under the employ of other European powers, meant that most of the investments went towards strengthening the city's defenses during the 16th and 17th centuries, while works of a religious nature were less important than they were in other Latin American colonies.

With the native population almost totally extinct, it was not necessary to undertake a mass conversion of the population to Christianity, nor to develop a strategy aiming at their ideological submission with the use of magnificent symbols of religious power.

On the other hand, the economic resources in the early centuries were very limited, making it necessary to construct modest buildings. The first church in Havana was a hut. When it became a building, however humble, the French corsair Jacques de Sores set it on fire without hesitation, destroying it along with the rest of the city on July 10, 1555. It was only rebuilt in 1574, although the church had, as the testimony of the period reveals, "neither paintings, nor books, nor ornaments, nor bells." The church was rebuilt and enlarged around 1666, dedicated to Saint Christopher, Patron Saint of the city, and, with the founding of the parishes of the Holy Spirit, Christ, Safe Voyage and the Guardian Angel, it took the name of Parroquial Mayor (Main Parish).

However, this hierarchical role did not provide any formal advantage to the church, so much so that it was stated that it looked on the outside "so plain that it seems a private home rather than the house of God." On June 30, 1742, a bolt of lightning struck the powder magazine of the ship *Invencible*, anchored in the harbor, causing an explosion that razed numerous building in the city, including the Main Parish.

The demolition of the ruins was hurried to build the Palacio de los Capitanes Generales on the same site in the Plaza de Armas. On December 9,1777, the Main Parish was transferred to a church then under construction near the small plaza of the Ciénaga by Jesuit fathers, who then saw it confiscated a short time before the expulsion of the Society of Jesus from Spain and her dominion. The church was transformed into a Cathedral and after the work of rebuilding and restructuring, begun in 1788, the small plaza around the church received its definitive name and gained importance and prestige.

The church forms a rectangle of 34 by 35 meters, divided internally by large pilasters in three naves and eight side chapels. The floor is in white and black marble tiles. The oldest chapels include one dedicated to the Virgin of Loreto, consecrated in 1755 and thus much earlier than the transformation of the small church into the Cathedral, and the chapel called the Sagrario, with its own entrance corresponding to the

parish linked to the Cathedral. The sculpture and goldwork of the main altar and its tabernacle in marble and precious metals were almost all produced in Rome in 1822 by the Italian artist Bianchini, who worked under the direction of the famous Spanish sculptor Antonio Solá.

Behind the main altar are three large frescoes by the Italian painter Giuseppe Perovani, as well as paintings by Jean-Baptiste Vermay. To understand better the value of the facade of the Cathedral, we can cite the eminent Cuban architecture historian Joaquín M. Weiss, who wrote: "Stylistically, this building goes much further than any of our other Baroque architecture." Weiss, in one of his best known works, calls attention to the cornice placed above the central door, which uses undulate forms and broken lines to express the freedom and the fantasy with which the facade of the great church was designed.

The Cathedral has thus come to the Cubans of today as a cultural and spiritual symbol of its past and as a synthetically expressive example of the country's colonial architecture. It is therefore not strange that the plaza, along with the buildings around it and the Cathedral that takes up its entire north side, is for many the most beautiful and representative image of Old Havana. In this plaza, between the streets of San Ignacio and Empedrado, is the Callejón del Chorro, a

One of the colonial buildings that surround Plaza de la Cathedral, the antique palace built by the marquis Aguas Claras. Today it houses the prestigious restaurant, bar and cafe El Patio.

The cupola of the Cathedral, viewed from the central nave near the main altar.

The main altar of the Havana Cathedral. The sculptures and goldwork that one can admire there were produced in Rome in 1820.

memory of other times when springs bubbled up there and the Zanja Real flowed, furnishing water to the people and the ships. One can still spot, in one of the walls along the Callejón, the original plaque that recalls: *This water was made to flow by Regiment Colonel Ivan de Texada. Anno 1592.*

The elegant buildings around the plaza are for the most part similar to many of the colonial buildings that can be found throughout the historic center and which have been copied in other Cuban towns. Generally, they are homes in the Moorish style with facades featuring monumental doorways, windows and balconies. They also feature spacious entryways and are usually characterized by an internal courtyard or patio surrounded by tile-covered porticoes.

These buildings were constructed like fortresses, endowed with a precise form. The interior was conceived for the comfort of the inhabitants, including the servants. On the corner of Empedrado and San Ignacio streets, near the Cathedral, is the building that belonged to the Marquis of Aguas Claras, today occupied by El Patio restaurant. From the restaurant's terrace, diners can appreciate a close-up view of the top of the church's famous facade.

The southern side of the plaza is occupied by the building that was the property of Don Luis Chacón, the governor of the island. It is said that some of the elaborate surfaces of this building, dating from the 18th century, are the most beautiful examples that can be found in Old Havana. Perfectly integrated within the setting of the plaza and with the scenario of this building is the Museum of Colonial Art, of the Havana National Historical Society, with an exhibition of furniture, lamps, porcelain and other objects and works of art that reflect the taste and customs of the period. Leaving the Cathedral and going left, one finds the home of the Count of Lombillo, whose family owned this palace in the 19th century, although in reality the building has occupied this site since the first quarter of the 17th century. Today the antique palace houses the Museum of Education, where visitors can admire, among the various displays, vivid testimonials of the literacy campaign carried out in Cuba in 1961. Next door, under the same portico, is the home of the Marquis of Arcos, another very representative colonial palace that is today the home of the Taller Experimental de Gráfica (Experimental Workshop of Graphic Arts).

The Plaza de la Cathedral is visited each day by thousands of tourists and Cubans, who enjoy the beauty of the area and its lively atmosphere. Traditional Cuban music, played by small bands, provide the background in the El Patio restaurant, with the echo of the singers and guitars drifting to the nearby Bodeguita el Medio. The Bodeguita specializes in Creole cooking and is famous throughout the world for its *Mojito de ron*, made of rum and mint, one of the favorite drinks of Hemingway. For many people, the restaurant begins or caps off a visit to the Plaza de la Cathedral.

Other religious buildings

Of the many religious structures built within the historic center of Old Havana, at least a dozen of them are worthy of mention. Following is a brief description of the most important churches.
In 1574 a small community of Franciscan monks settled in Havana, where ten years later they began work on the church and convent of Saint Francis of Assisi.

At the far end of the plaza on the opposite side of the Cathedral is the palace that today houses the Museum of Colonial Art, run by the Havana National Historical Society. A visit to the museum is obligatory for an understanding of the atmosphere and customs of the city in times past.

The attractive central courtyard of the Museum of Colonial Art is surrounded by galleries. Note the lowered arches on the ground floor and the lack of arches on the top floor.

The church and its monastery, located near the present day streets of de Oficios and Brasil (Teniente Rey), were reconstructed and enlarged numerous times in the course of almost two centuries, until in 1738 the complex reached its present shape.

A short distance from the harbor and surrounded by an irregularly shaped plaza, the Franciscan building was for a long time the most elegant church of colonial Havana, characterized by an unusual and tall bell tower, by far higher than the towers of any other church in the city. Starting in 1841, when the Spanish government took over the property of the religious orders, the church was put to many uses, for the most part quite different than its original purpose, until the present day. At present, the Minor Basilica, thanks to its extraordinary acoustics, is used as a hall for concerts and chamber music.

As if it were a sort of relic among the buildings of colonial Cuba, the surviving section of the church of San Francisco de Paula, once a part of a women's hospital, is worthy of a visit. Located on a small traffic circle near the bay, at the meeting point of the streets of Leonor Pérez (Paula), San Isidro and San Ignacio, the impressive bulk of the antique church stands in view of the numerous drivers who crowd this spot with their cars. The dome of the church of San Francisco de Paula is particularly interesting for its pre-Churrigueresque Baroque style. Inside of the church are the remains of the great Cuban violinist Claudio José Brindis de Salas, while the hospital that stood next to the church was the scene of several pages of the first Cuban novel, *Cecilia Valdés*, by Cirilo Villaverde.

Among other religious buildings of Old Havana is also the Seminary of San Carlos and San Ambrosio, whose construction dates back to the 18th century and

A room recreating 19th-century fashion, with sets of medallóns. To the left is a piece in the Louis XVI style. The small tree in mother of pearl on the table is an example of the works produced in jails and convents. The crystal chandelier is French.

Bedroom with furnishings from the second half of the 19th century. Note the bronze cradle and the opaline chandelier.

Nineteenth-century dining room. In the glass case to the right are examples of China that belonged the Creole bourgeois of the era.

therefore prior to that of the Cathedral. The experts maintain that the only merit of its exterior is the doorway; however, they agree with admiration on the quality of the interior, with its quadrangle delimited by galleries and its fine examples of doors and finely carved wooden grilles, with high quality reproductions still on display. In addition to its many architectural qualities, the Seminary was for many years, during the entire colonial era, an important center of lay education in which numerous important national patriots developed their culture and conscience.

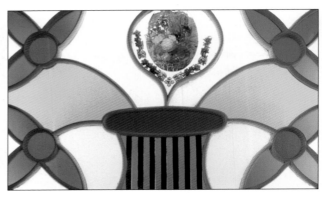

Very characteristic of Creole crafts is the production of applied glass above doors and outside-facing windows. These decorative elements serve to let in softer light. This late 19th-century skylight with decals is in translucent and ground crystal.

Another example of Creole glass art, which, as opposed to the usual lead crystal, uses glass and wood for the decoration. This is another 19th-century skylight with decals, in translucent and ground glass.

Cuban glass art began in the mid 18th century, continuing till the end of the 19th century. Similar works can be admired throughout the country in the homes of the middle classes and aristocracy. This piece was found in a home dating from the second half of the 19th century.

Flower holder with its pedestal.

This English porcelain flower holder is in the Museum of Colonial Art.

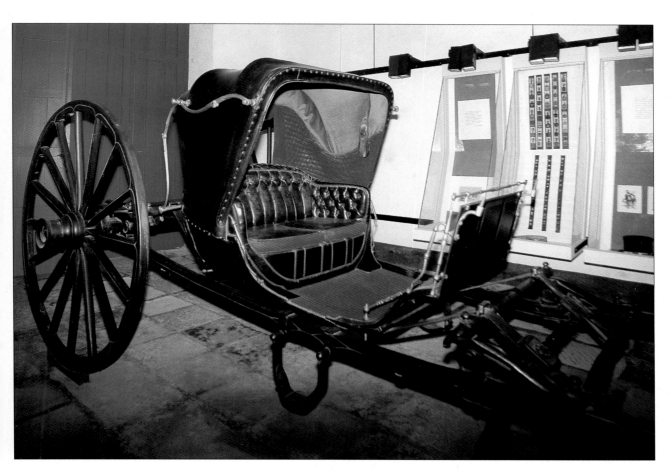

The most luxurious means of transportion in the 19th century was the gig. This carriage, on display in the Museum of Colonial Art, was manufactured in Cuba.

A back view of the gig exhibited in the Museum of Colonial Art. Its beauty and excellent craftsmanship can be admired.

The Plaza de San Francisco hosted, during the earliest settlement of Havana, the public market. The first mention of it dates back before 1559.

The church of San Francisco was first built starting in 1584. Rebuilt in 1738, the church and its convent are important sites in Cuban history.

The church of San Francisco de Paula, on Avenida del Puerto, is characteristic of the Cuban Baroque style of the first half of the 18th century.

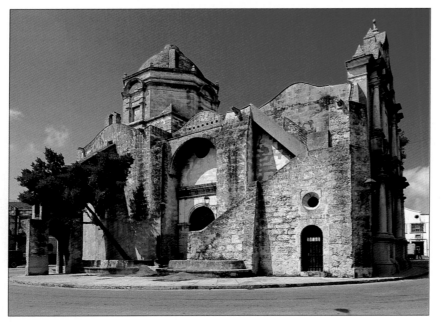

The Seminary of San Carlos and San Ambrosio was rebuilt in the 1950s in a style defined by some experts as Cuban Neo-Baroque.

In 1836, the center of the Plaza de San Francisco was graced with this beautiful fountain, la Fuente de los Leones. The fountain is the work of Italian sculptor G. Gaggini, who also made the famous Fuente de la India, or the Noble Habana.

The facade of the Seminary of San Carlos and San Ambrosio clearly recalls the facade of the Cathedral, although without the same solemnity of the latter.

General view of the Castillo de la Real Fuerza, the first military fortress built in Cuba and one of the first in the Americas.

Partial view of the moats of the Castillo de la Real Fuerza. The design of the fortress, like that of the other colonial forts of Havana, was influenced by the style and the architectural concepts of the Renaissance.

The only tower of the Castillo de la Real Fuerza. Atop the cupola is La Giraldilla, the symbol of the city of Havana.

THE MAIN FORTS OF HAVANA

The treasures that Havana accumulated in the course of its economic development thanks to its strategic port was reason enough to siege the city for pirates, corsairs and fleets of the European powers, who fought over the centuries with Spain and disputed her rule in many areas of the Americas. The danger that threatened Havana became evident a very short time after the founding of the city, when the first inhabitants had to suffer numerous attacks and sackings, including that of the terrible French corsair Jacques de Sores, who in 1555 destroyed all that stood in his way. The Crown then became convinced of the immediate need to provide Havana with military protection able to repel any attack and decided to begin fortifying the city.

Castillo de la Real Fuerza

The first of these military fortifications was begun in 1558 and finished in 1577. A side of Plaza de Armas was chosen for its location, probably because this was where the main settlement was situated and the highest city officials lived. The Castillo's wide moat, its appearance of a medieval castle complete with drawbridge and its thick walls set over a polygonal plan give it the impression of being a seemingly impregnable fortress.

In little time, however, the Castillo de la Real Fuerza showed its inability to sustain enemy attacks. The fact that it was built in a somewhat less than fortuitous location from a strategic standpoint, and the lack of combat stations which had become evident from the outset, immediately provoked heated polemics. The composition of the first garrison that occupied the Castillo was also laughable. In fact, the garrison consisted of that blend of cultures which, in the course of the following centuries, would constitute one of the salient features of the Cuban national identity: of the 50 men, 19 were born in Portugal, two gunners were

Flemish and one was German, and, to further increase the ethnic diversity, the first drummer of the Castillo de la Real Fuerza was an old Negro slave. The unmistakable landmark that this fortification provided for the city was made even more conspicuous when between 1630 and 1634 a small tower was added to one of the highest points of the complex and was topped with one of the enduring symbols of Havana: the *Giraldilla*, a bronze statue molded and cast in 1630 by Havana artist Gerónimo Martín Pinzón and depicting a woman watching over the city and in the distance far beyond the harbor.

Despite the building's lack of functionality as a fort, it was never demolished, even though several attempts were made to raze it. The Castillo de la Real Fuerza ended up being used as barracks and offices during the colonial era and as the headquarters of several institutions during the 20th century. At present it houses the National Museum of Artistic Ceramics. The Castillo de la Real Fuerza, despite its lack of military activity, gained a place in the coat of arms that King Philip II presented to Havana when he granted the settlement the title of city in 1592.

First placed as pennant in 1630, the original Giraldilla *was toppled by hurricane winds in 1926. Today it is kept in the Municipal Museum, with a copy taking its place atop the tower of the Castillo de la Real Fuerza.*

The front of the Castillo de la Real Fuerza, with the drawbridge. At present, the fortress houses the National Museum of Artistic Ceramics.

The esplanade in front of the entrance of the Castillo de la Real Fuerza. The cannons of different caliber and range were manufactured between the 18th and 19th centuries.

A detail of the stairway that leads to the embattled terraces that held the artillery of the Castillo de la Real Fuerza.

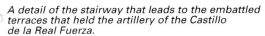

Castillo de los Tres Reyes del Morro

Another fort of Havana that has a place in the city's insignia is the Castillo de los Tres Reyes del Morro (Castle of the Three Kings of Morro), the second fort built in Havana. It was completed in 1630, after 40 years of work. Its construction was commissioned by the Italian engineer Gian Battista Antonelli, and the location chosen for it was a rock promontory that closes the line of the bay on its northern side. From here, the view of the sea was better and its location was farther from the dwellings than that of the previous fort of Real Fuerza. These facts, in addition to its superior arms, led people to believe that once the new castle would be in operation, the city would have become an impenetrable bastion.

A century later, however, at the dawn of June 6, 1762, a multitude of vessels belonging to the large British fleet was spotted on the horizon from here. The fleet had regrouped near the Florida peninsula and was sailing southwards in the direction of Havana, whose territory it was evidently intent on

In front of the Morro, the small fort of La Punta dating from 1630. It was built on the norternmost point of the bay channel to create a line of crossfire on enemy ships. Pictured is a frontal section of one of its bulwarks.

View of the Castillo de la Real Fuerza from the fortress of the Cabaña.

Panoramic view of the Castillo de los Tres Reyes del Morro, built at the beginning of the 18th century.

capturing. After 44 long days of siege and despite the tireless defense of the populace, Havana fell into the hands of the English. The final blow dealt by the British was the placement of several mines among the stones of the Morro, where the valiant defenders of the city's last bulwark fought.

The English remained on the island for a year until an agreement was worked out with Spain to exchange their dominions, with the latter regaining possession of its "most faithful Havana" and the former receiving the North American territory of Florida. The conquest of Havana by the English not only deeply shook Spain's military predominance and political control of the island, but—a fact that was even more terrible for the city—it spelled the decline of commerce and traffic that ended once and for all economic monopoly of the Spanish. The Creoles began to look more attentively towards other horizons and to understand gradually that independence from Spain would be fundamental for the economic and political interests of Cuba.

The bitter lesson learned from the period in which Havana was no longer under the firm control of Spanish colonial power could not, however, allow itself to be repeated. For this reason, one of the first plans of the Crown for Cuba, once it had reestab-

Entry to the loophole gallery that provides access to the Castillo de los Tres Reyes del Morro and view of bastions and moats, now dry, that circle the fortress.

The Castillo del Morro and part of the lighthouse, seen from the fortress of the Cabaña.

The lighthouse of the Morro, the oldest in Cuba, was built in 1845. The lighthouse is 48.5 meters high, and provides a view of 43.5 nautical miles.

Detail of the sentry box placed on the extreme of the Austria Bulwark, one of the two main bulwarks of the Castillo del Morro. Below is the entrance to the loophole gallery.

Old barracks inside of the Castillo del Morro. In the background are the lighthouse and the coastline of Havana.

lished its control over Havana, was that of rebuilding the Castillo del Morro and adding another fortification to the city. In 1845, a new tower, reaching 48.5 meters above sea level, was built on a hill and inaugurated at the Morro. The light of this tower, like those before it—though not as tall or elegant, but of equal utility—served to pinpoint the harbor to ships approaching the bay at night, while to departing ships it signaled their last farewell and lit their path to the open sea.

The jar room, original clay vessels where rape-seed oil was stored to keep the lighthouse lit at night.

"The Evolution of Mapmaking" in the Hall of Great 15th and 16th Century Voyages of the Castillo de los Tres Reyes del Morro.

Reproduction of a caney, a native dwelling with walls of tree branches and a conical roof of palm branches. Inside of the crude dwelling exhibited in one of the rooms of the Castillo del Morro is a hammock and original work and hunting tools as well as some semies (idols) worshipped by the first inhabitants of the island.

Vestibule of the Hall of Great Voyages. The displays provide an interesting overview of the geographic knowledge at the time Christopher Columbus came to Cuba.

Esplanade of the Twelve Apostles, located on a low area of level ground overlooking the entry to the harbor.

Main entrance to the Castillo de San Carlos de La Cabaña, built by the Spaniards at the end of the 18th century following the end of the English takeover of Havana. Partial view of the now dry moats.

Castillo de San Carlos de La Cabaña

Several small castles, such as the Atarés and del Príncipe, are located within the city of Havana. But the third most important fortification of the city and the largest in the Americas was the Castillo de San Carlos de La Cabaña, built next to the Morro and completed in 1774. "A work that cost so much, one should be able to see it as far away as Madrid," said King Carlos III, according to the chronicles, when he was informed of the cost of Havana's new castle. Fourteen million pesatas, a true heresy, were paid from the city's coffers to construct the new defensive structure of the city, whose size and solid appearance should have at least awed potential enemies. And that was apparently the case, since once all the cannons of the Cabaña had been forged and emplaced, they remained silent. Or at least all of them except for one, used for the ceremony of the Cañonazo, a tradition that began in the 16th century in another part of the city and today takes place in the Cabaña.

It is said that the blast indicated the opening and closing of the walls of the city and of the port, which was made unapproachable by a chain of enormous links

The Plaza de Armas inside of the Castillo de San Carlos de La Cabaña.

View of the main road inside of the Cabaña and of the old barracks, now transformed into exhibition halls for ceramic goods, military history and antique arms.

Battery of 21 bronze cannons cast in Seville in the 18th century, used to protect the entry to the bay from the fortress of the Cabaña.

strung across the channel. The opening shot occurred at 4:30 a.m. and the closing shot at 8 p.m. So it was at least until the occupation of the United States, when the first shot was abolished and the second shot moved to 9 p.m. The well known signal thus changed its time and function, but it continued nevertheless to sound each evening, with the exception of the last years of the Second World War (1942-45), when it was decided that Cuba shouldn't waste

Church of the Castillo de La Cabaña.

Sentry box in the north bulwark of the fortress of San Carlos de La Cabaña.

Historical reenactment in period uniforms. Every evening at 9 o'clock, a cannon shot is fired from the Cabaña, at it was in the times when the gates to the walled city were shut.

gun powder for shooting blanks. The rule was undoubtedly over cautious, and the populace managed to overturn it through persistent pressure.

Today the large fort next to the Morro, completely restored and perfectly preserved, is the headquarters of the Parque Histórico Militar Morro-Cabaña, where visitors can look over the past and admire one of the most beautiful views of Havana from the high walls.

Photograph of Commandant Ernesto Che Guevara taken on January 3, 1959, the day in which he took command of the fortress of the Cabaña several hours after victoriously entering Havana at the head of a column of his soldiers.

CHE GUEVARA AT THE CABAÑA

On January 2, 1959, late at night, Che Guevara reached Havana for the first time in an olive-green Chevrolet, together with several jeeps and trucks that carried the 400 guerrillas of his military column. The Cuban Revolution was on the verge of triumphing and the Argentinean Ernesto Guevara, first commander designate by Fidel Castro, who himself was in the Sierra Maestra, had orders to take the second most important fort of the capital, the Castillo de San Carlos de La Cabaña, while commander Camilo Cienfuegos, his friend and disciple, was given the task of occupying the Columbia barracks, the headquarters of the troops of a dictatorship whose leader had already fled.

The city, occupied by the troops of the Movement of the 26th of July after that January dawn, breaks into celebration. Everyone wants to meet the mythical Argentinean soldier with the thin beard who had joined Fidel Castro in Mexico to take part in the expedition of 82 men pledging to be "free or martyrs," that man of 31 years of age with a tough and at times ironic temperament, the guerrilla who dealt the decisive blow to the dictatorship in the city of Santa Clara.

But Che, his arm in a sling after the battle of Santa Clara, moves unhesitatingly towards the fortress of the Cabaña. The sentinels of the old regime, under the watchful eye of the militia men on the outside of the encampment, fear for their lives, and keep hold of their weapons. Without hesitation, Che walks into the fort, which for five months will serve as the fighter's headquarters. At dawn of January 3 he calls the 3,000 soldiers before him and says: "The guerrillas must learn discipline from you, and from them you must learn how to win a war."

From that day onwards, Che lived in the Cabaña in a building constructed at the end of the 19th century, where the governor of the fort had resided. With time, the old palace, where the asthmatic fighter received constant visits by journalists, celebrities, friends and war comrades, took on a sort of air of sacredness. At the end of the 1980s, it was made into a museum which houses a large exhibit of objects belonging to the "Heroic Guerrilla," as the Cubans usually call Che. The original weapons that Che used in the mountains of Cuba, in the forests of the Congo and in the Bolivian Andes, his eye glasses, and his camera that he kept during the first years of the revolution, are some of the objects that allow us to imagine the person, along with the photos and the papers that trace the steps of the life of this emblematic man: his childhood, his travels as a young man across Latin America and the most important revolutionary events that he took part in.

The plazas and the barracks of the Cabaña were not only the scene of his short military career before being named the president of the National Bank of Cuba and, subsequently, the Minister of Industry. During the five months in which he was the head of the garrison, the fortress was transformed into a key seat of revolutionary theory and practice.

Immediately after his arrival he in fact created the Military Cultural Academy, which followed up on a practice that he had begun in the Sierra Maestra, despite the urgency of the war: literacy and education of his troops, most of whom were farmers who had never attended school. He instituted several workshops, the so-called "Cabaña Libre," in the fields around the old fortress, where the soldiers produced artisan goods to make themselves self-sufficient. He also created the nursery school "Los Barbuditos" in which children listened to the enterprises of the war heroes and where they were taught to load and unload old rifles, which they did before modest fiestas for new soldiers. Today, from the window of his perfectly conserved office in the Cabaña, it is possible to see the same Havana that Che contemplated for the first time, perhaps with a certain amazement, on that dawn of January 3, 1959.

The office used by Che Guevara in the Castillo de La Cabaña during the first five months of the triumph of the Cuban Revolution.

HAVANA BEYOND THE WALLS

Like the old European feuds, Havana was protected by a ring of walls built between 1667 and 1680 along its western side. The defensive reasons that had led to the construction of the system of castles and forts to defend the coast also motivated the construction of the walls, which, already at the beginning of the 18th century, began to make expansion of the city a problem, while their military and strategic significance diminished.

The area inside of the walls, at the time inhabited by about 80,000 people, had become too small and lacked a coherent urban plan able to harmonize all the interests and needs of a city that was assuming a role that was among the most important and promising in the Americas. The Alameda de Extramuros, a tree-lined avenue connected to the Muralla, was one of the first signs of the urban expansion of Havana. The Habaneros wanted shade and fresh air to enjoy their evenings in the nearly 1,000 carriages that then circulated in the city, and for this reason, according to a 1760 account written by the first historian of the city, those who lived near Havana suddenly began to prefer spending their leisure time in the spacious area that extended around the Muralla, where until then military activities had taken place.

Beyond the walls, a new city was to rise over the centuries starting in the 1700s. To be exact, it was between the years of 1834 and 1838, while general Don Miguel Tacón was governor, that Havana had its first urban and

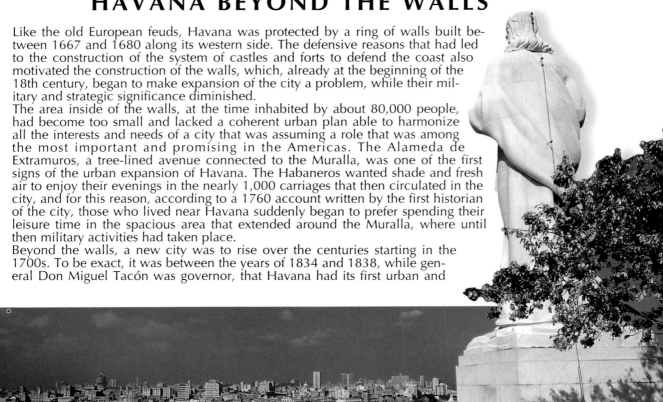

architectural plan, which mostly focused on the area around the walls. One of the works in the plan was the famous Tacón Theater, inaugurated in great pomp in 1838, as described by the countess of Merlin: "This theater is both rich and elegant; ... the governor's box is larger and more ornate than that of the king in other theaters. Only the leading theaters of the great European capitals can compete with the beauty and decorations, the splendor of the lighting, the elegance of the spectators all in yellow gloves and white trousers, of that of Havana."

This theater was one of the most obvious symbols of economic well-being that the country was enjoying. Thanks to the trade in slaves, to scientific progress, and to access to new markets, especially with the United States, Cuba began to become an important producer of sugar at the end of the 18th century. The profits of this industry began to fill the coffers of the municipal treasury and made many men rich. Most of these were Creoles, as the natives of Cuba were called, and they in turn began to demand independence for the island. Out of the need to maintain political hegemony, the government of the island, represented by Tacón, promoted new works to demonstrate by their magnificence the advantages of the defense of Spanish interests in Cuba.

If up until then most of the buildings of the old city were religious, military or residential, during the process of urban development in Havana there appeared a great profusion of new works for a wide variety of uses, such as markets, theaters, cafes, ice cream parlors, ballrooms, shops, hotels, villas, the railroad station, boardwalks, avenues ... a whole network of city services.

The Christ of Havana looking towards the city. Sculpted in white Carrara marble, it is 15 meters tall. Thanks to its position at the top of the hill of the Cabaña, the statue stands 79 meters above sea level.

View of the Havana waterfront from the Castillo de San Carlos de La Cabaña. The domes of the Capitol and of the Presidential Palace (Museum of the Revolution) stand out.

This Christ by sculptor Jilma Madera has blessed the city of Havana since 1958.

Monument to Generalissimo Máximo Gómez. In this view it is possible to see the tunnel running beneath the bay, connecting its two sides.

Main entrance to the old Presidential Palace, built in 1918 and today home of the Museum of the Revolution.

Still preserved in front of the Presidential Palace is this section of the walls of Havana: the sentry box of the Guardian Angel bulwark, or the Angel Bulwark.

Small factories were also built, the result of the modernization of the urban economy. Still existing among these are the tobacco works, a product that distinguished itself among all of those that were exported from Cuba and which today continues to be unequaled. The residential buildings began to express more obviously the economic differences of the new owners. Along with the luxurious homes that gave an air of opulence to Havana, one could encounter houses that were much more modest, conserving the typical austerity of the city of the 16th and 17th centuries. These homes continued to be found in quarters far from the new city beyond the walls, close to what is today called Old Havana. The program undertaken by Tacón was so extensive that many experts agree that there was not another of the same breadth until almost a century later, during the republican period under the government of dictator Gerardo Machado. With the arrival of the 20th century and the end of the Spanish colonial regime on the island, a new period began for the development of Havana. Despite the years of war against Spain (1868-78, 1895-98), the Cubans could not achieve real independence: as soon as the Spanish surrendered their domination, another foreign power flung itself on the country. In 1898, the United States intervened in the Spanish-Cuban conflict to win a future protectorate in Cuba, which enabled them to establish the basis for a new kind of domination, neo-colonial, that lasted for the entire first part of the 20th century.

The foreign influence over the economic, political and cultural life of Cuba also left its mark on the architecture of Havana. The Baroque style, for example, which was predominant during the Spanish colonial period, was considered a symbol of the defeated regime and rejected. The fashion shifted towards the most diverse stylistic currents: Neo-Renaissance, Neo-Baroque, French Art Deco or Art Nouveau from the Catalan masters. In the first years of the 20th century, Neo-Classicism also had a marked influence. The style was one that recalled the republican civil virtues from the Roman tradition, exalted by the French Revolution and assimilated by its heirs, the most developed European societies and especially the United States.

It was thus that monumental works were built in Havana, many of them for civic purposes, with appearances typical of those found in the great European capitals, if not, as in some cases, imitations of existing buildings.

The Hall of Mirrors, the former receiving room of the Presidential Palace.

The second and third floors of the Museum of the Revolution seen from their broad marble staircase.

A room in the Museum of the Cuban Revolution, in one of the halls that once belonged to the Presidential Palace.

Presidential Palace (Museum of the Revolution)

Inaugurated in 1920, this civic work is the most eclectic building among those used by government offices. It was the seat of the executive power starting in 1959 and for this reason the building is of great historic importance, which is further reinforced by the fact of its having been the scene of one of the most shocking successes of those years.

In 1956, a group of young University of Havana students attempted to attack the palace and execute Fulgencio Batista to end his dictatorship. Bullet marks are still visible today on the walls, in addition to a large collection of objects and documents pertaining to the event. Today the palace houses the Museum of the Revolution, one of the most important in the country, which covers the entire history of Cuba from its discovery up to the present.

Photographs, objects and documents of the revolutionary history of the Cuban people exhibited in the rooms of the museum.

*The Capitol of Havana. Its elegant dome,
at some 91 meters, can be seen from many areas
of the city.*

The Capitol Building of Havana

Completed in 1929, the Capitol was the result of the most extraordinary architectural imitation. However, it is possible to identify some innovations in the Cuban tradition, such as the inner courtyards, very similar to those that abound in the buildings of Old Havana, and the use of precious domestic hardwoods.

Beneath the large dome, which is the axis of the entire building, stands the third tallest statue in the world (17 meters): a Minerva Protectoress, symbol of the Republic, in cast bronze. At her feet, in a small display case, is a diamond—with obvious reference to the Arc de Triomphe in Paris—that marks the beginning of the Carretera Central, the first road to cross the island and built under the Machado government.

The two symmetrical lateral pavilions at the base of the dome were for the legislative bodies of the House and Senate, incarnating the liberal conception of the balance of power.

Their interiors have rich decorative elements in diverse styles of great opulence and an almost idolatry rhetoric, based on the image of the Republic which had just been constituted.

Since 1962, the Capitol has been the headquarters of the Academy of Sciences of Cuba and more recently of the Ministry of Science, Technology and the Environment, as well as other institutions that have relations with the world of information and scientific documentation. The main floor, with its 15 fine halls and carefully restored galleries, is the home of the Capitol Center of Havana, in charge of organizing meetings, fests and tours of the majestic building.

The old Centro Gallego, today the Grand Theater of Havana, one of the most beautiful architectural monuments of the city.

Statue of José Martí, dominating the Parque Central. It was the first statue erected in honor of the "Apostle" of Cuban independence.

Centro Gallego (Grand Theater of Havana)

In the spot originally occupied by the Tacón Theater in the 19th century, Havana exhibits another of its most beautiful monuments. The Centro Gallego, today the Grand Theater of Havana, was built facing the Parque Central in 1912 and has one of the richest exteriors of any building in the capital. With its spiral scrolls and turrets embellished with statues of angels and Muses, the Centro Gallego endowed the areas of old Havana beyond the walls with a strong cosmopolitan sense and became one of the unequivocal incarnations, as Alejo Carpentier wrote, of "this style without style that in the long run, by symbiosis, by amalgamation, becomes a Baroquism."

Carpentier was a well-known Cuban novelist, who also had architectural training. He often looked intently to discover the hidden treasures of Havana, and to direct distracted eyes at that which, although obvious, is sometimes missed: "little by little, from the multi-colored, from the extreme, from the elaborate that incarnates itself in realities very different one from the other, have arisen the constants of a general appearance that distinguishes Havana."

Parque Central

Starting from the 19th century, the Parque Central has become the Habaneros' most popular location. Situated where colonial Havana blends with the new city, this tree-filled plaza constituted the beginning of the famous Paseo de Extramuros. But with the frenetic urbanization that took place in this section of the city at the beginning of the century, the park gradually lost its central location, even thought it still is an important geographic, historic and cultural point of reference.

In the middle of the plaza, with its lovely gardens of flowers and majestic ceibe trees, there originally stood a statue of Queen Isabella II, which was toppled with the end of Spanish dominion. Subsequently, the first statue in Cuba dedicated to José Martí was placed there, which still occupies the spot.

Among the buildings on Avenida del Malecón is the so-called "Caryatids Building" with its design typical of the eclectic style combining Neo-Classical and Deco elements. The building houses the Center of Spanish Culture.

This small palace with its eclectic design was strongly influenced by the styles of the Italian Renaissance, quite atypical in the context of Old Havana. In was built in 1905. Today it is home to the National Music Museum.

The Hotel Nacional of Cuba, emblem of Havana, built in only 13 months in 1930, is one of the most beautiful and luxurious in the country.

El Vedado is now considered the most central area of the city of Havana.

MODERN HAVANA

The long avenue known as Malecón de La Habana is a sort of balcony that looks out at the waters of the Gulf of Mexico. A seafront avenue extremely popular with Habaneros, the Malecón begins in front of the Castillo de la Real Fuerza and ends in modern Havana, near the Torreón de La Chorrera, a military construction of 1665.

In the section running along El Vedado are many buildings from the 1950s, with a marked American influence (from Art Deco to modern monumental), that co-exist with eclectic buildings of the Cuban middle classes from the beginning of the century. Starting from the 1930s, this area of the city began to become one of the city's most attractive neighborhoods due to its shining modern image, and it continues to be so today. The popularity that El Vedado enjoyed prompted the most powerful families to seek isolated and peaceful areas towards the west in which to build their houses. Thus, neighborhoods like Miramar arose, which today contains the most sumptuous examples of Cuban architecture from the first half of this century.

Host to some of the most important personages in the world, the Hotel Nacional conserves photographs of some of these guests in the so-called Hall of Fame.

52

Hotel Nacional

The biggest and most luxurious hotels in Havana were built in El Vedado following a tourism development plan promoted by the Mafia in the United States. The plan aimed at transforming the seafront of Havana into one enormous Las Vegas casino.

The Hotel Nacional, where a multitude of persons linked to international crime met and lived, was built in 1930 on a hill a short distance from the Malecón. Special care has been taken to conserve the original decorations in the majestic building. Its several levels, embellished with small and lovely artistic mosaics, its marble columns and scagliola that support the roof, and its public areas have all been preserved to look as they did when the building was completed, endowing the Hotel Nacional with a very special appearance.

Celebrities from the international worlds of politics, culture, science and athletics have passed through the large doors and the gardens of this building, which is a fascinating and sober example of the Spanish plateresque style.

The monument to José Martí, national hero of Cuba, dominates the Plaza de la Revolución. The viewing terrace at the summit of the obelisk, at some 139 meters, is the highest point in Havana and offers a fine panorama of the entire city.

Beneath the monument of the José Martí Memorial.

Plaza de la Revolución

One of the most emblematic and majestic constructions of contemporary Havana is the monument to José Martí, a mass of gray marble reaching 139 meters in height. Built between 1958 and 1959, this enormous monument pays homage to the national hero of Cuba, rising above the historic Plaza de la Revolución. The Plaza has witnessed the largest political rallies of the Cuban people, many speeches by Fidel Castro and one of the masses of Pope John Paul II. The modern monumental architecture surrounding the Plaza de la Revolución houses the main political-administrative institutions of the country, as well as the José Martí National Library and the National Theater. In front of the monument, on the facade of the Ministry of the Interior, an immense metallic structure holds the image of the venerated commander Che Guevara.

The area of the Memorial also provides information on the construction of the Plaza and on the most important events that it has witnessed.

The seat of the José Martí National Library, founded in 1901. The design of the building (modern monumental) makes it the most characteristic among the buildings on Plaza de la Revolución.

Behind the José Martí Memorial is the building housing the most important offices of government: the State Council, the Council of Ministers, and the Central Committee of the Cuban Communist Party.

The most famous image of Che in the world, a unique work reproduced on the facade of the building that at the beginning of the Revolution housed the Ministry of Industry, which was directed by Che, and which today houses the Ministry of the Interior.

The Avenida Paseo, one of the most beautiful and greenest avenues of Havana. It begins at the foot of Plaza de la Revolución and crosses the area of El Vedado, ending at the Malecón and the sea.

HEMINGWAY IN HAVANA

It was almost without realizing it that the giant, reddish, childish individualist with his short pants and sunglasses came to live in Cuba. Havana, where he arrived for the first time in 1928 for a 48-hour tropical vacation, would become the only really stable residence of the fickle literary genius, Ernest Hemingway. All of his homes, more or less temporary, tell the story of 22 years of his intimate presence in this city, which strangely was never the explicit setting or protagonist of his novels.

It was never love at first sight between Havana and Hemingway. His first visits to the Cuban capital did not seem to show anything more than his desire to partake in the simple pleasure of fishing for impressive specimens of swordfish and needle-fish in the mysterious currents of the Gulf of Mexico. But later his sentimental relations with this country and especially with this city became lasting and profound. In 1956, when he was awarded the Nobel Prize for literature, he announced in perfect Spanish his decision to donate the prize to Our Lady of the City of Cobre, the Patron Saint of Cuba.

At the beginning, there were only relatively short trips. During his fishing expeditions, Hemingway came to know the humble seamen who lived in Cojímar, a fishing village east of Havana.

Among the "good folk," who ended up calling him "Papa," were to be many of his future and faithful friends. Some of them, who became protagonists and characters in novels such as The Old Man and the Sea and Islands in the Gulf, removed the bronze propellers from their boats when they heard of the suicide of the illustrious writer and friend and commissioned a sculptor to make the expressive statue that was placed in the old square of Cojímar, in front of the dock where Hemingway used to moor his boat, the Pilar.

The modest Plaza Hemingway was the first in the world to be given his name.

The Pilar, built in 1934, was skippered by Gregorio Fuentes, a fisherman and friend of the writer. Fuentes received the boat in Hemingway's will, and in 1961 he donated it to the Hemingway Museum.

Before departing as war correspondent on the front of the Spanish Civil War, Hemingway already had three favorite places for his sojourns in Havana: the Floridita, a bar-restaurant today famous throughout the world for its shellfish specialties and its Daiquiris, a cocktail that the novelist promoted all over the world; the Creole restaurant la Bodeguita del Medio, where he used to drink a Mojito and chat with friends; and a room on the last floor of the Hotel

The Finca Vigía, a few kilometers from Havana, has remained the way its owners left it in 1960. It is now the Hemingway Museum.

The trophies of animals hunted by Hemingway in Africa, Europe and the United States are displayed throughout the house.

Ambos Mundos, near Plaza de Armas and the Cathedral of Havana, which upon his return from Spain became his favorite hiding-place for writing.
But when Hemingway decided to spend long periods in Cuba, the Ambos Mundos became too popular with his friends and admirers. In 1939, his third wife found an ideal place where the novelist could finish For Whom the Bell Tolls: a home 15 kilometers from the city that was called Vigía, in the village of San Francisco de Paula.
The house was built between 1886 and 1887 by a Catalan architect. The luminous building, which, in the words of its owner "seemed like an old boat," took on much of the fame and myth of Hemingway. He spent almost all of his evenings in the large living room sitting in his favorite armchair, reading a good book and with the mobile bar designed by him always within reach.
In Vigía he wrote more than half of his works and

threw parties for Hollywood celebrities, boxers, bullfighters, authors and artists. But Hemingway had a characteristic that was particularly liked by the Cubans: he didn't act like a Señor, a master.
His home was open to whoever wanted to come in or was in need, humble as the person may be.
With the triumph of the Cuban Revolution in 1959, despite the pressures of the United States on Cuba, Hemingway remained in Vigía (now a museum) until he left for Spain in 1960. There he came down with his fatal illness that did not allow him to return to his island, and in 1961 he committed suicide in the United States.
This great American who preferred to live in Cuba, apparently distant from all the turbulent events of the island and dedicated to the pleasures of writing novels and drinking whisky, forever won the hearts of Cubans with one of his last comments, given to a journalist: "We will win. We Cubans will win."

The dining room, a simple room furnished with Spanish style country furniture. Here too the most notable decorations are the animal trophies: a kudu, an oryx from Kenya and a pronghorn antelope from Idaho.

The bedroom of Hemingway and his wife Mary.

The writer's private room, where he usually worked and rested. On top of the bookcase is his Royal typewriter. Hemingway always wrote standing up.

Under the play of shadows cast by the flowers of the climbing plants covering the trellis is the cistern for the house's water supply.

Kept in the gardens of Finca Vigía is one of the museum's exhibits, the Pilar, the boat used by Hemingway for his frequent fishing expeditions in the waters of the Gulf.

A short distance from the Cathedral of Havana is one of the finest Cuban restaurants, La Bodeguita del Medio. It walls, which almost have no room left for visitors to leave signatures, poems and comments, its characteristic rustic furnishing, and its typical Creole fare have made La Bodeguita a universally known spot.

The restaurant/bar Floridita, one of the places in Havana preferred by Hemingway. It is said that the American writer used to say: "My Mojito at the Bodeguita, at the Floridita my Daiquiri."

2,000 years ago *the Ciboneyes Indians already lived on the island. Their presence lasts until about 1515, when they were exterminated by the Spanish conquistadors.*
Other indigenous groups of differing levels of development also populated the island before its discovery.

1492 (October 28) *Christopher Columbus lands on the coast of Bariay, in the northeast of the island. He names the land Juana, in homage to the first child of the Catholic king and queen, Ferdinand and Isabella. Tobacco was already being cultivated by the natives.*

1509 *Sebastián de Ocampo charts the territory, demonstrating that it is an island.*

COLONIAL ERA

1510 *Diego Velázquez begins the conquest and colonialization that concludes in 1514. The Spanish bring cane sugar to cultivate.*

1512 *In the zone of Baracoa, the cacique Hatuey rebels.*
After several months of resistance against the Spanish, he is captured and condemned to die, burned at the stake. This was the first show of struggle for freedom on Cuban territory.
Founding of the first village, which was named Nuestra Asunción de Baracoa. In the next two years, other villages were also founded: San Salvador de Bayamo, la Santísima Trinidad, Sancti Spíritus, San Cristóbal de La Habana, Santa María de Puerto Príncipe (Camagüey) and Santiago de Cuba. Each village had a governing organ know as Cabildo.

1526 *One hundred and forty five African slaves are brought to Cuba. This barbarous and repugnant practice of human commerce continued until the 19th century, with the purpose especially of developing sugar production in the country.*

1537 *Starting from this date, corsairs and pirates attack Cuban villages. In 1555, the French corsair Jacques do Sores occupies, sacks and destroys Havana.*

1558 *The process of fortifying Havana begins, which will last until well into the 17th century.*

1561 *Spain organizes fleets of war ships to protect mercantile vessels sailing from the Americas towards the city. It also establishes Havana as the mandatory meeting place of these fleets, providing the city with an economic boom and transforming it into the exclusive center of legal commerce. The inland population is forced, for survival, to illegally trade with corsairs and pirates from England, France and Holland.*

1608 *The first work of Cuban literature is produced: the poem Espejo de paciencia, by Silvestre de Balboa, a native of the Canary Islands.*

1701 *From now until 1720, 100 factories for the production of sugar are established on the outskirts of Havana.*
Others are also built in the center of the island. The production of tobacco also increases.

1728 *The first University of Cuba is founded in Havana.*

1762 *The English take Havana on 12 August. Their rule lasts eleven months and has favorable repercussions on the economic life of the city.*
Large quantities of English goods flow into the city, as do numerous slaves who are put to work in sugarcane plantations.
The islands grows wealthier thanks to the production of sugar and tobacco and other export products.

1763 *With the Treaty of Versailles, England returns Havana to the Spanish, receiving Florida in exchange. The Spanish monarchy begins to practice illuminated despotism.*

1781 *Trade with North America is authorized on the condition that Spanish merchants do not participate. The United States gradually become the biggest purchaser of Cuban sugar.*

1789 *Free trade of slaves is established.*

1790 *The Papel Periódico de La Habana is founded, the first newspaper published in Cuba, for a reading audience of agriculturists, merchants and culture lovers.*

1791 *Cuba takes control of the sugar and coffee markets, which previously belonged to Haitian growers, whose plantations were destroyed by war. The cultivation of sugarcane expands, becoming the most important Cuban export crop. Slavery increases.*

1793 *The Real Sociedad Económica de Amigos del País (The Royal Economic Society of Friends of the Country) is founded, with the goals of promoting the development of the island's main economic activities and increasing education and culture.*

1810 *The first independence conspiracy takes place under the direction of Román de la Luz and Joaquín Infante, who drafts the first project of a Cuban constitution. Among the most important independence conspiracies is that of the Soles y Rayos de Bolívar (1821-1828), in which the lawyer and first great Cuban poet José Maria Héredia was implicated and sent into exile.*

1812 *The abolition conspiracy movement led by the freed Negro slave José Antonio Aponte is discovered. The objectives of the movement are the abolition of slavery, social equality and the destruction of Spanish tyranny.*

1824 *From now until 1825, Félix Varela publishes in Philadelphia and New York "El Habanero," the first Cuban revolutionary newspaper. Because of his political ideology, Varela comes to be considered the precursor of ideas on independence, of love for the homeland and liberty.*

1826 *Alexander von Humboldt, the German scientist considered to be the second discoverer of Cuba, publishes the Political Essay on the Island of Cuba, the first scientific work on the geography of the country.*

1837 *The first railway in Cuba is built, before one is built in Spain, to transport sugar.*

1838 *The Tacón Theater is inaugurated in Havana. It is considered one of the most luxurious and important in the world at the time.*

1850 *Giuseppe Garibaldi arrives in Havana, remaining for several months.*

1853 (28 January) *José Martí is born in Havana. He becomes the founder of the Cuban Revolutionary Party and organizer of the War of Independence; poet, literary critic, journalist, diplomat and excellent writer.*
He is considered the Cuban national hero. He dies in battle on 19 May 1895.

1868 (10 October) *Carlos Manuel de Céspedes, recognized by Cubans as the "Father of the Nation," frees his slaves and sets off the first war against Spanish dominion. The war lasts ten years.*
(20 October) *What is to become the Cuban national anthem is sung for the first time in the city of Bayamo, taken by the patriots. National Culture Day is celebrated each year on this date.*
(4 November) *Spanish troops are charged by machete-armed patriots led by Máximo Gómez.*

1869 *The Assembly of Guáimaro gathers in April and approves the first Constitution.*

1878 (10 February) *The Zanjón Pact is signed: a group of military and civic leaders surrender to the commander of the Spanish troops.*
(15 March) *Major General Antonio Maceo refuses to accepts the Zanjón peace treaty, which he considers a "disgraceful surrender" that stains the dignity of the Cuban people. This act, of great revolutionary import, is historically known as the Protest of Baraguá.*

1883 *Investment of United States capital begins on the island, first in the industries of sugar and minerals, and then in other sectors. By now, control of the Cuban economy can be said to be in the hands of the United States.*

1892 (10 April) *José Martí founds the Cuban Revolutionary Party, which unites all the forces in the country to lead the winning struggle against Spanish domination.*

1895 (24 February) *The War of Independence begins, to whose organization were dedicated José Martí, Máximo Gómez and Antonio Maceo.*
(19 May) *José Martí, leader of the revolution, falls in uneven combat against the Spanish troops. His mortal remains are in the cemetery of Santa Ifigenia in Santiago de Cuba.*

1896 (7 December) *The lieutenant general of the Liberation Army Antonio Maceo, the "Bronze Titan," dies in combat at San Pedro, near Punta Brava in the province of Havana.*

1898 (15 February) *Spain has now virtually lost the war. In the harbor of Havana, the United States battleship, the Maine, explodes, giving the pretext to the Americans to militarily intervene in the conflict, with the objective of preventing the liberation of Cuba. In December, Spain and the United States, without the presence of the Cubans, stipulate a peace accord, signing the Treaty of Paris.*
The United States military occupation of the island begins, lasting for about three years.

1901 The new Constitution is approved, in which the United States imposes an amendment, the Enmienda Platt, by virtue of which the United States denies the sovereignty and self-determination of the Cuban populous. In the same year, the National Library is founded.

NEO-COLONIAL REPUBLICAN ERA

1902 (20 May) The first Cuban president takes office. Cuba becomes a neo-colonial republic subordinated to the interests of the United States.

1906 (November) The second intervention of the United States takes place through 1909. Cuba's economic and political dependence on U.S. imperialism increases.

1921 Cuban José Raúl wins the title of world chess champion.

1924 With the painting Gitana Tropical by Victor Manuel, Cuban contemporary painting is born.

1925 The Cuban Communist Party is constituted. Among its founders is Carlos Baliño and Julio Antonio Mella. The dictator Gerardo Machado receives orders to repress the people's revolutionary movement.

1929 (10 January) Julio Antonio Mella is assassinated in Mexico by order of Machado.

1930 Nicolá Guillén, recognized as the national poet, publishes his first collection of verse: Motivos de son.

1933 (12 August) A general revolutionary strike brings about the fall of the Gerardo Machado dictatorship.
In the same year, the greatest Cuban novelist, Alejo Carpentier, author of, among his many works, El reino de este mundo, El siglo de las luces, Recurso del método, publishes ¡Ecué-Yamba-O!, his first novel.

1940 (5 July) The new constitution is approved, which, thanks to the participation of communist delegates, includes articles favorable to the interests of the Cuban populace. In the same year, Fulgencio Batista becomes president of the Republic.

1948 The National Ballet of Cuba is founded, whose most important member is the prima ballerina Alicia Alonso.

1952 (10 March) Batista attempts a military golpe supported by imperialists to destroy the government of Carlos Prío. Thus begins the bloodiest dictatorship suffered by the Cuban people.

1953 (26 July) Fidel Castro, at the head of a group of youths, assaults the Moncada barracks in Santiago de Cuba. At the trial, conducted behind closed doors, Castro delivers his self-defense, History will absolve me, which will become the political program of the Revolution.

1956 Fidel Castro and his comrades go into exile in Mexico to reorganize the struggle. There, Castro meets Ernesto Che Guevara. With 82 men, they return to Cuba aboard the boat Granma. The guerrilla war begins in the Sierra Maestra.

1958 The final battles of the War of Liberation take place. The dictator Batista flees the country on 31 December.

THE REVOLUTIONARY ERA

1959 (1 January) The Cuban Revolution triumphs. Fidel enters victoriously into Havana on 8 January.
(4 July) The Casa de las Américas is founded, a cultural institution that was to bring together the most important Latin American intellectuals. The literary award Casa de las Américas is considered to be among the most prestigious in international circles.

1960 (8 August) The nationalization of the country's economic resources begins.

1961 (3 January) The United States break diplomatic relations with Cuba, and the policy of economic embargo begins.
(16 April) The socialist character of the revolution is proclaimed.
(17 April) One thousand five hundred mercenaries of Cuban origin living in the United States land in the Bay of Pigs (Bahía de Cochinos) and attack the Playa Girón and Playa Larga. But the invasion is repulsed in only 72 hours.
(22 December) The literacy campaign reaches its apex, with a million

Cubans learning how to read and write. With an act celebrated in Plaza de la Revolución, Cuba is declared Illiteracy Free Territory.

1962 October Crisis. The president of the United States, John F. Kennedy, orders a naval blockade against Cuba and asks the USSR to remove the nuclear warheads placed in Cuban soil. Cuba maintains its intransigent stand during these events.

1963 (6 February) The government of the United States makes the naval blockade against Cuba official.

1965 (1 October) The Central Committee of the Cuban Communist Party is constituted. In occasion of this event, Fidel Castro reads the Leave of Absence extended to Che, in Congo to organize the guerrilla war.

1967 (8 October) Ernest Che Guevara falls wounded in battle against the Bolivian army and is killed the following day.

1972 The Nueva Trova movement has its beginnings, led by songwriters and singers Silvio Rodríguez and Pablo Milanés.
In the same year, middleweight boxing champion Teófilo Stevenson wins his first Olympic gold medal, which he will also go on to win in the 1976 and 1980 Olympics.

1975 The first Congress of the Cuban Communist Party takes place in December.

1976 (15 February) The democratic-socialist Constitution of the Republic of Cuba is approved by popular referendum.
During the Pan-American Games of Montreal, runner Alberto Jantuorena wins two gold medals in the 400 and 800 meters.

1978 The 10th World Youth and Student Festival is held in Cuba.
Novelist Alejo Carpentier wins the important Miguel de Cervantes literary prize.

1979 (3 September) The 6th Conference of Non-Aligned Countries begins in the Palacio de Convenciones in Havana.
(3 December) The 1st International Festival of New Latin American Cinema is inaugurated.

1980 (4 April) The first Soviet-Cuban space flight takes place.

1990 Because of the fall of the blockade of socialist countries and the disintergration of the USSR, Cuba loses 85 percent of its foreign trade, to which the exacerbation of the U.S. embargo is added.
The country lives an economic crises which is followed by the so-called Período Especial.

1992 The crises worsens, especially after the U.S. government promulgates the Torricelli Law against those countries intending to break the economic blockade against Cuba.
Cuban poet Dulce María Loynaz wins the Miguel de Cervantes literary prize.

1993 Cuban poet and essayist Eliseo Diego wins the Juan Rulfo Prize in Mexico for his body of literary works.

1996 The government of the United States approves the Helms-Burton Law to destroy Cuba economically and re-establish a capitalist regime on the island.

1997 In the summer of this year, 11,000 young people from all over the world arrive in Cuba to celebrate the 14th World Festival of Youth and Students.
(14 October) After being found, the remains of Ernesto Che Guevara and his comrades depart from the airport of Valle Grande, in Bolivia, to return to Cuba and be laid to rest in Santa Clara.
The athlete Ana Fidelia Quirot, after numerous triumphs in international championships and after a period of recovery following an accident, becomes the world champion in the Athens Olympics in the 800 meters.
In the same games, Javier Sotomayor, world record holder in Salamanca in 1993, wins the gold medal in the high jump.

1998 (21-25 January) The visit of Pope John Paul II is the first ever by a pope. His ecumenical mission includes the celebration of four masses in the cities of Santa Clara, Camagüy, Santiago de Cuba and in the Plaza de la Revolución in Havana.

Contents